AF381710

Alla mia famiglia e ai miei amici
Per la vostra generosità, gentilezza ed il vostro sostegno
Sono molto fortunato di avervi nella mia vita ogni giorno

Ciao!

Sono Antoine, un francese di 26 anni originario del sud ovest della Francia, tra Toulouse e Dax.

Ho vissuto a Milano per tre anni, dal 2019 al 2021, mentre studiavo design del prodotto al Politecnico, in Laurea Magistrale. Grazie a questa opportunità, ho scoperto una città che mi affascina per diversi motivi, tra cui la sua architettura a metà tra passato e modernità, sobrietà ed eccesso, insieme alla pluralità dei suoi quartieri, la sua cultura del design, la sua passione per il calcio, il cibo e la sua musica indipendente.
WQuesti anni hanno avuto un vero impatto su di me. Primo, ho scoperto cosa volessi fare: lavorare nel design. Ma Milano mi ha anche dato l'opportunità di incontrare gente di culture completamente diverse ed imparare da loro ad avere una visione del mondo, forse, un po' più completa.

L'obiettivo di questo libro non è creare la guida perfetta di Milano, ma condividere i miei posti, e mostrare la città dal mio punto di vista, quello di uno studente straniero in Erasmus. Questo progetto è anche l'occasione per sviluppare il mio stile grafico.

Sono veramente impazzito per questa città e questo libro è una maniera di dichiararglielo. Spero che leggerlo vi faccia attraversare la stessa esperienza.

Buona lettura

Antoine

THANK! YOU

for supporting this project
with your purchase

INDICE

Milano In Fretta — 01 — p.8

Milano Per Quartiere — 02 — p.12

Outside Milano — 03 — p.74

Indie Italiano — 04 — p.84

PICTOGRAMS

Da Vedere

Da Bere

Da Mangiare

Da Festegiarre

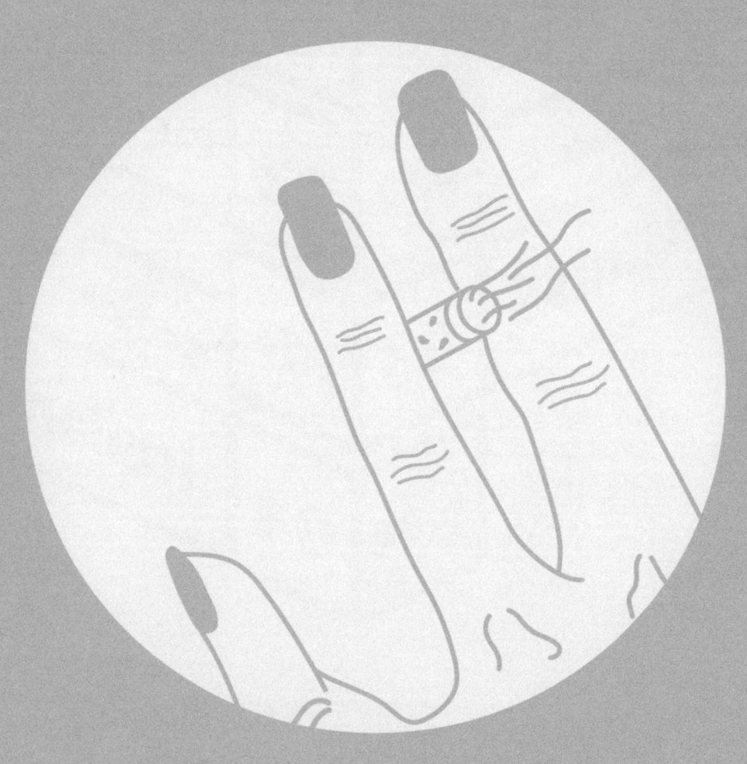

Milano
In Fretta

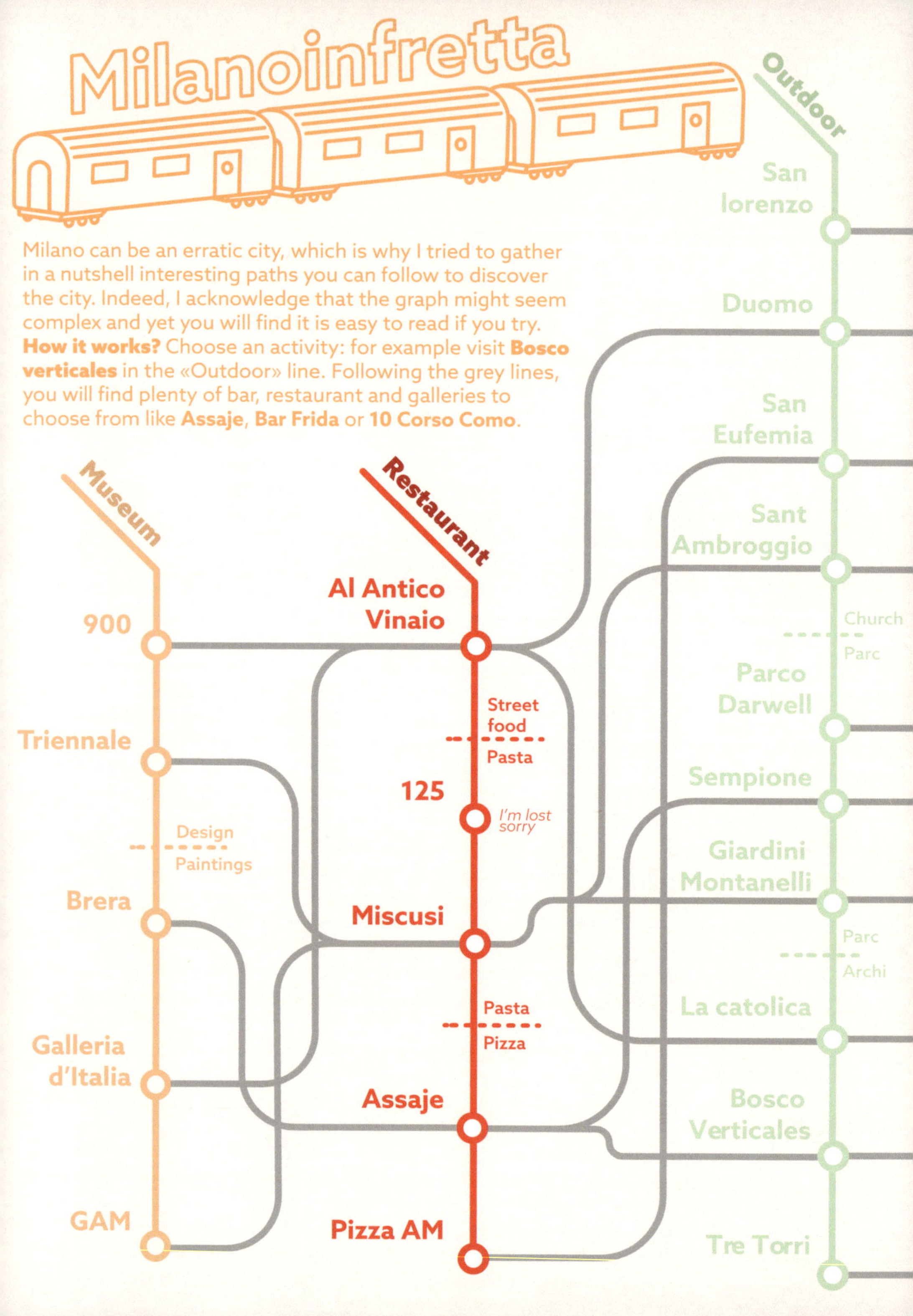

Milanoinfretta

Milano can be an erratic city, which is why I tried to gather in a nutshell interesting paths you can follow to discover the city. Indeed, I acknowledge that the graph might seem complex and yet you will find it is easy to read if you try. How it works? Choose an activity: for example visit Bosco verticales in the «Outdoor» line. Following the grey lines, you will find plenty of bar, restaurant and galleries to choose from like Assaje, Bar Frida or 10 Corso Como.

Museum
Restaurant
Outdoor

San lorenzo
Duomo
San Eufemia
Sant Ambroggio
Church
Parc
Parco Darwell
Sempione
Giardini Montanelli
Parc
Archi
La catolica
Bosco Verticales
Tre Torri

900
Triennale
Design
Paintings
Brera
Galleria d'Italia
GAM

Al Antico Vinaio
Street food
Pasta
125
I'm lost sorry
Miscusi
Pasta
Pizza
Assaje
Pizza AM

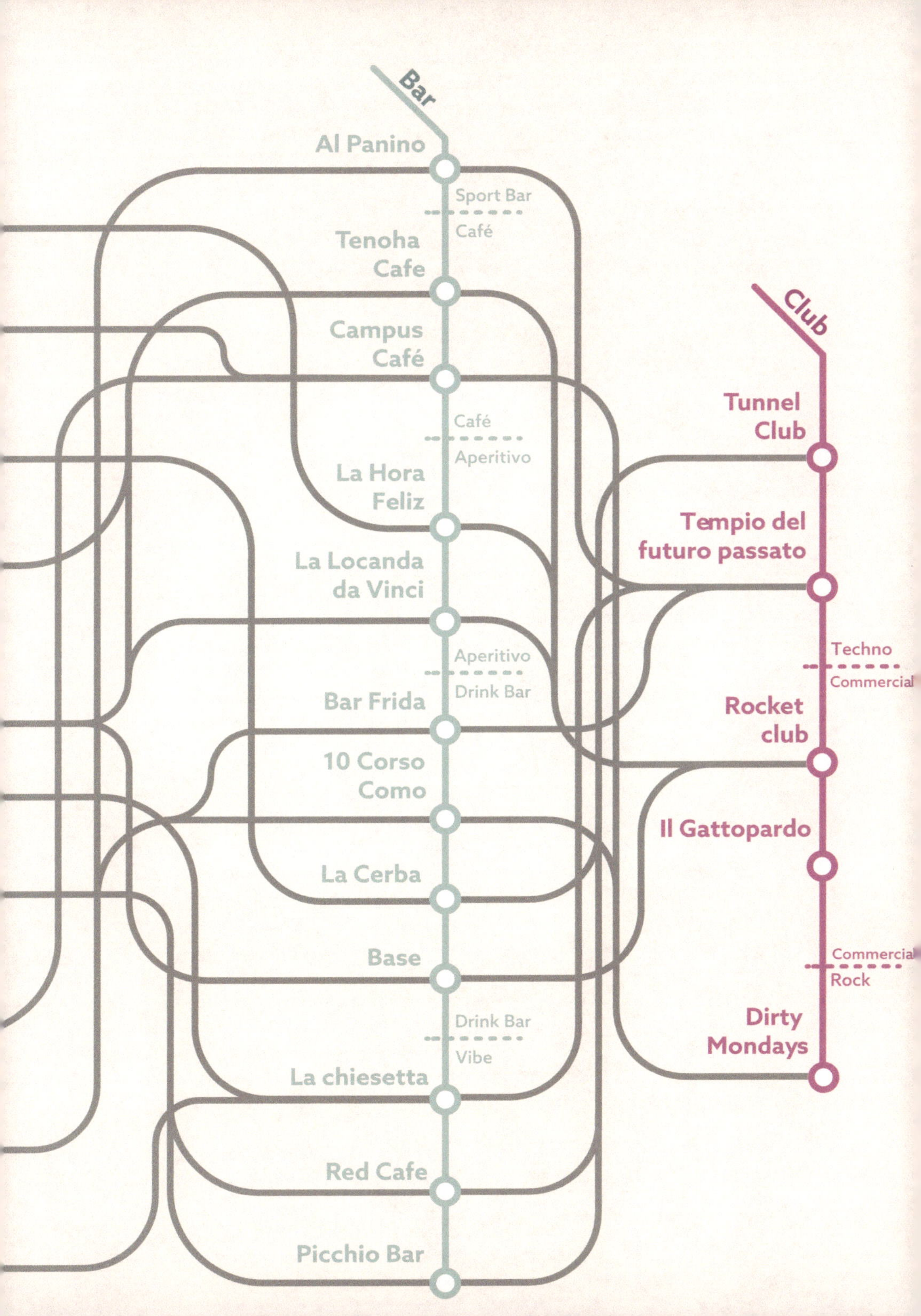

Bar
Al Panino
Sport Bar
Café
Tenoha Cafe
Campus Café
Café
Aperitivo
La Hora Feliz
La Locanda da Vinci
Aperitivo
Drink Bar
Bar Frida
10 Corso Como
La Cerba
Base
Drink Bar
Vibe
La chiesetta
Red Cafe
Picchio Bar
Club
Tunnel Club
Tempio del futuro passato
Techno
Commercial
Rocket club
Il Gattopardo
Commercial
Rock
Dirty Mondays

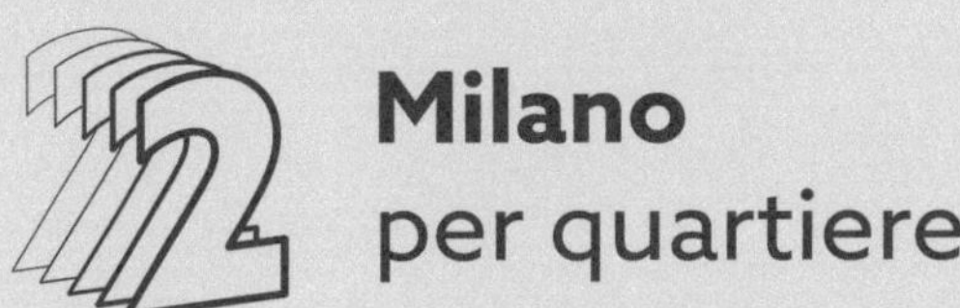

Map

9. **Bovisa** p.62

3. **Isola** p.28

5. **Monumentale** p.40

6. **Buenos Aires** p.46

10. **Tre Torri** p.68

8. **Lambrate** p.58

2. **Brera** p.22

7. **Navigli** p.52

1. **Centro** p.16

4. **San Lorenzo** p.34

CENTRO
5
9
14
2
1
4
13
6
10
11
7
3
8

I **Centro** is home to the city's most famous emblem: the **Duomo**, an incredible Gothic church crowned by **La Madonnina**, which keeps a constant watch over the city. This district encapsulates the rich history of the Lombardian capital, with **La Scala**, **La Galleria Vittorio Emmanuele II**, and il **900**.

Due to its popularity, this part of the city can often be quite crowded. Therefore, the best time to enjoy it is right after leaving the Nepentha club from **Dirty Mondays**. I can assure you that the Duomo will be yours at that time!

But don't worry, there are still some cozy and intimate places in the city center. Take Via Palazzo Reale to reach the **Universita degli Studi**, where you can grab a coffee at the **Campus bar** or something to eat before enjoying it in the **Giardini della Guastalla**.

To See

① Il Duomo

This gothic building is the symbol of the city. Even if the interior is really dark and modest, I have been amazed by the wonderful Milan view on the rooftop.

P.za del Duomo

③ La torre Velasca

With its distinctive «mushroom» shape, it stands as a modern symbol of milanese brutalism.

Piazza Velasca, 3/5

② Galleria Emmanuele II

This shopping arcade is another iconic symbol of Milan. Aside of upscale shops, the legend tells that turning 3 times on mosaic bull's nuts will brings you luck.

P.za del Duomo

④ 900

Museum with a rich collection of Italian modern art. Reach its top at night to have a stunning view on piazza Duomo and the magnificient Lucio Fontana neon sculpture. This unique combination of modern art and panoramic view of Milan's iconic landmarks is not to be missed.

P.za del Duomo, 8

⑤ Galleria d'Italia

I really enjoyed this museum which gathers both modern (Fontana) and classic collections (Hayez, Induno, De Albertis). In the same square, you can also catch a glimpse of the famous theater La Scala.

Piazza della Scala, 6

⑥ Chiesa San Bernardino alle Ossa

I love the area between this church and the university. There are many bars, restaurant and it is surprising to find such a quiet area compared to the effervescence of the Duomo. If you have some spare time, have a look at this church inside.

Piazza Santo Stefano

⑦ Università degli studi di Milano

Maybe one of my favorite places in Milan. The building is organised in cloisters (ideal to have a quiet break from city's hustle and bustle) and provides a calm environment to study.

Via Festa del Perdono, 7

⑧ Giardini della Guastalla

Cute and relaxing parc in the center of Milan. Perfect to read or enjoy the food from uni area.

Via Francesco Sforza

⑨ Quadrilatero della Moda

This district gathers iconic fashion brands. It is pretty interesting to see that much opulence in such a restricted area. But it is quite amusing to get some free champagne if you fake being rich.

Via Monte Napoleone

 **To EAT**

⑩ All'Antico Vinaio

Originaly from Firenze, this street food place offers delicious sandwiches made with good Italian charcuterie at affordable prices! Special mention to «L'Inferno».
For a complete experience, grab your panini and enjoy it on Piazza Sant'Alessandro's stairs.

Via Lupetta, 12

 **To DRINK**

⑪ CAMPUS CAFE

Old school cafe facing the università degli studi, I fell in love with the retro interior decoration. Perfect place to enjoy a good Italian coffee with some traditional butter biscuits.

Via Festa del Perdono, 10-14

⑫ Vanilla Gelati Italiani

Very nice gelateria close to the Duomo.

Via Pattari, 2

⑬ DIRTY MONDAYS

Fans of 2000s pop/rock music, this is definitely the ultimate spot to enjoy a night out in Milan. The underground club offers a warm and inviting athmosphere. Be sure to check the unique design of the DJ set. After the party, do not miss the chance to snap a solo picture in front of the Duomo just before sunrise.

Nepentha Club Piazza Armando Diaz, 1

⑭ Le Banque

Fancy club in the center of Milan. Commercial music mainly. While it may not be considered the absolute best club in Milan, it's a great choice for a fun Erasmus party.

Via Bassano Porrone, 6

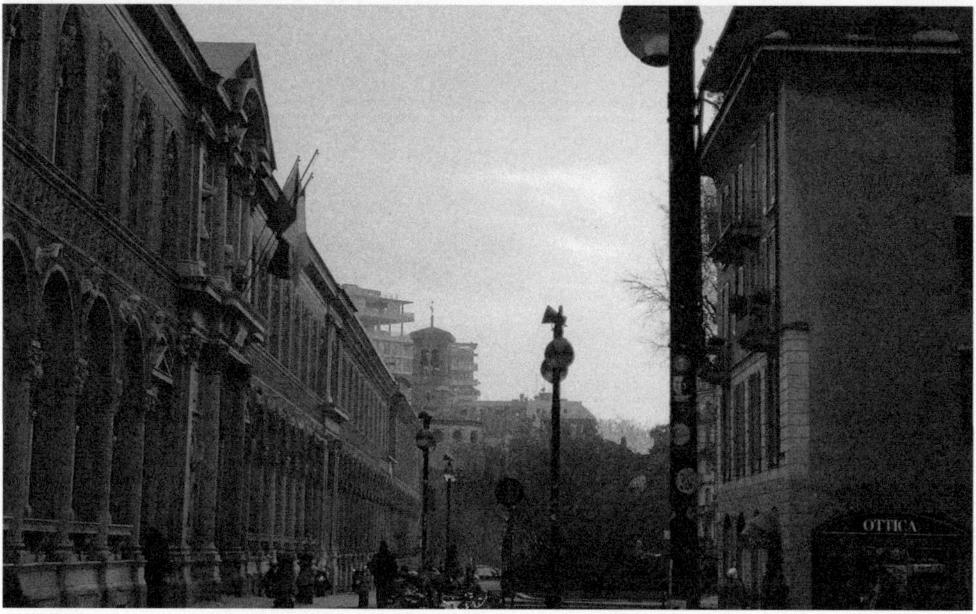
OTTICA

19 RICALCOLO
NM1 NOTTURNA
6 DEVIA E SAL

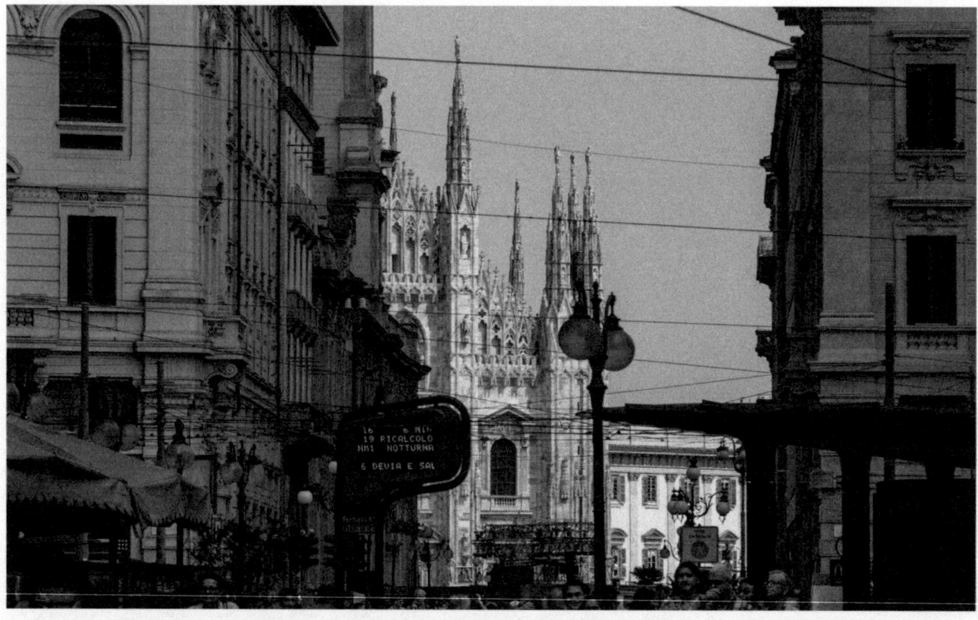

MARTINI

BRERA
13
11
2
1
14
15
3
9
8
7
10
6
4
5
12

Milano is known for its design culture, and Sempione and Brera are a testimony of this heritage. Beside the iconic **Castello Sforzesco**, the park hosts **La Triennale**, a design / modern art museum to discover the story of italian design culture.

Sempione is also a very nice park to savor late summer afternoons, on the grass drinking homemade cocktail. If you still interested by Italian design, have a walk to Brera district and **Via Solferino,** which gathers one of the best design furniture brands. For the classic art lovers, do not miss the opportunity to visit **La Pinacoteca di Brera** to admire Il Bacio di Hayez. If you continue north, you have two drinking options after this long walk: cocktails in the intimate and hidden **10 Corso Como** or a beer in the lively **Al Panino** to watch a football game.

To See

① Parco Sempione

Really nice park in the center of Milan. Perfect for a run or get some drinks with a bunch of friends. The park also hosts Castello Sforcesco, a really nice castle to pass by but I can't tell about the museum, I have not seen it.

Piazza Sempione

② Arco della pace

At the end of the park, you will be able to notice this majestic arch. This is a cool place to chill during summer (you might catch up an open air silent disco or APE event if you are lucky!).

Piazza Sempione

③ Triennale

Modern art museum gathering the products that made italian design history. Beside the permanent collection, the building hosts interesting temporary exhibitions (photo, cinema…). In addition, during summer open air cinema session are organised in the garden.

Viale Emilio Alemagna, 6

④ Pinacoteca di Brera

Human scale museum of classical paintings. I really did enjoy the diversity of style and artist. A truly must-see museum in Milan. Special mention to «Il Bacio» di Hayez or «Cena di Emmaus» del Caravaggio. At the entrance, the Napoleon statue and the peaceful garden make the place even more special.

Via Brera, 28

⑤ Brera

In my opinion, one of «the most Italian» districts of Milan by its charming tiny and colorful streets. Really pleasant to walk around in the search of a coffee or good pastry.
Take the opportunity to visit la Chiesa del Carmine or la Parrocchia S. Simpliciano for their elaborated facades.

Piazza della Scala, 6

⑥ Via Solferino

Nice area gathering the best Italian design brands. I really enjoyed just wandering around and explore the shops.
At the beginning of the street, have a look to the beautiful Chiesa Parrocchiale di San Marco.

Via Solferino

⑦ Porta Garibaldi

Take a moment to see the Microsoft office / Feltrinelli Fondation construction… The architecture is quite unique because of its unusual tiny width. It is also very fun to be able to notice the internal decoration thanks to numerous bay windows.

Via Francesco Sforza

To **DRINK**

⑧ 10 Corso Como

Really nice concept place!! On the first floor, you will find a fancy bar behind a bunch of plants, with a clothing store. Then, go upstair to check the design/architecture library. If it is not enough to catch your attention, you have also temporary exhibitions displayed (drawing/photo/graphic design…)

Corso Como, 10

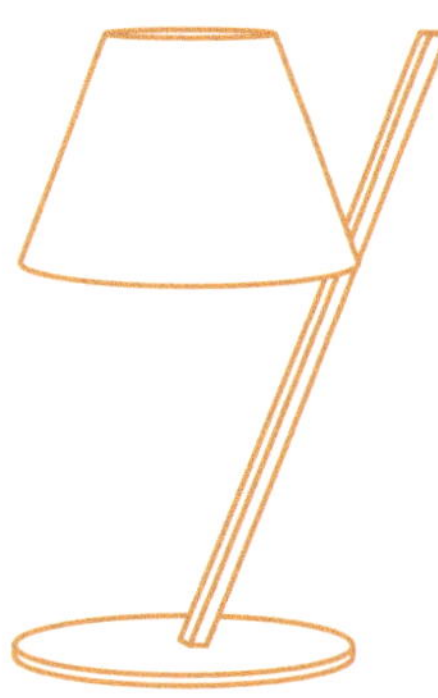

⑨ Al Panino

One of the best bars to watch football games in Milan. Authentic «tifosi» plus great piadina/focaccia participate to the great athmosphere of this place to watch game of Inter or Milan. Even better during a derby!

Viale Francesco Crispi, 5

⑩ Chinese Box

This part of Corso Garibaldi has a bunch of aperitivo places and the Chinese Box is a good one to admire the Murale Artistico di Gucci. The facade changes often with some nice graphical proposition.

Corso Garibaldi, 104

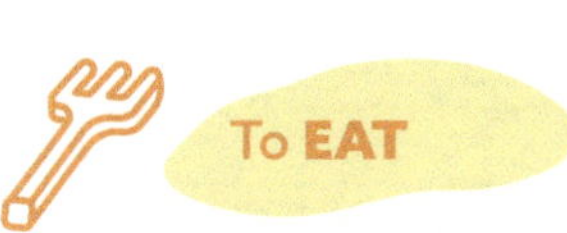

To **EAT**

⑪ Banghrabar

Classic aperitivo place for a rather cheap price for such big cocktails.

Corso Sempione, 1

⑫ Salsamenteria di Parma

Very nice and cozy osteria next to Sempione.

Via Festa del Perdono, 7

⑬ **Deseo**

Very nice aperitivo place with a wide range of food to offer. Outside, you have a beautiful view on Arco della Pace.

Corso Sempione, 2

To **Party**

⑭ **Just Cavalli**

I have never been to this club but I have heard that for eramus nights, there are good vibes and an outdoor dancefloor inside Sempione.

P.za del Duomo

⑮ **Old Fashion**

Classic commercial club. However, the outdoor dancefloor is very appreciated when days get longer and warmer.

Palazzo dell'Arte, Viale Luigi Camoens

GUCCI
ANIMA
zona
traffico limitato
divieto di transito a:
eccetto:
controllo
con telecamera
zona
traffico limit
serie
30
30

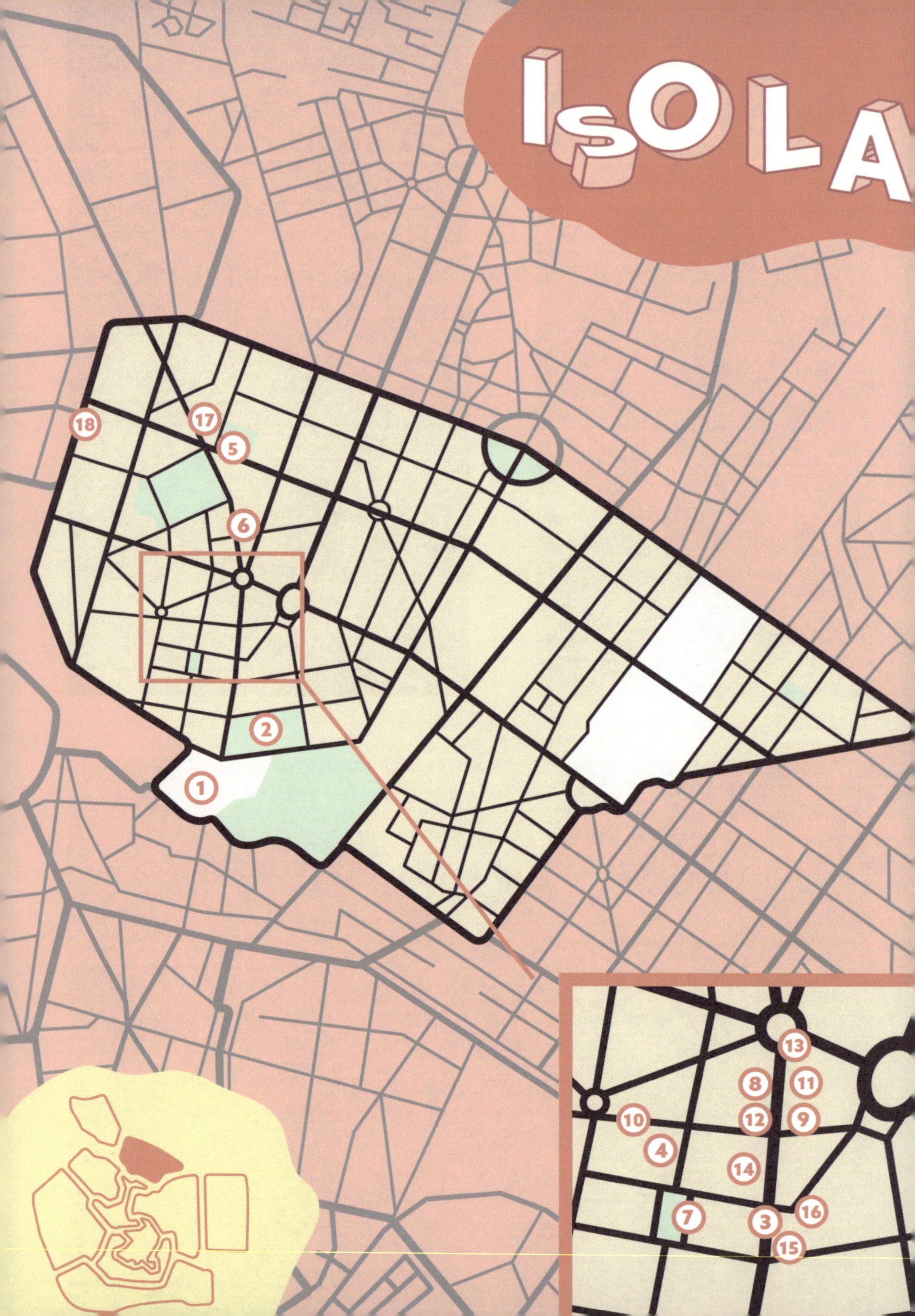

ISOLA
18
17
5
6
2
1
13
8
11
10
12
9
4
14
7
3
16
15

Isola is my favorite district of Milan. Ok, I might not be so objective since I lived in this area for 2 years, it shows Milan for what it really is; through a contrast between modernism and classic architecture, the presence of a well established design culture and great food.

On one hand you can admire the futuristic contructions around Garibaldi with **Bosco Verticales** or **la torre UniCredit**. Whereas further north, you will discover a calm and cozy area full of nice bars and restaurants. For instance, you can start by having a dinner on **Via Borsieri**, drink some cocktails around the cute **piazzale Carlo Archinto** and finish in **Alcatraz** until the end of the nigth.

To See

① Piazza Gae Aulenti

I really liked to have a walk around these modern buildings. The building design is amazing and it is quite well integrated inside the city.

Piazza Gae Aulenti

② Bosco Verticales

While Duomo is the symbol of Milan, Bosco Verticales is clearly the emblem of the modern side of the city. It is really interesting to see how much the plants hide the building structure. These apartments are integrated inside the BAM park, cool place to chill and have an home made aperitivo. You also have some events (concert exhibition…) organised inside the park. A must see!

Piazza Sempione

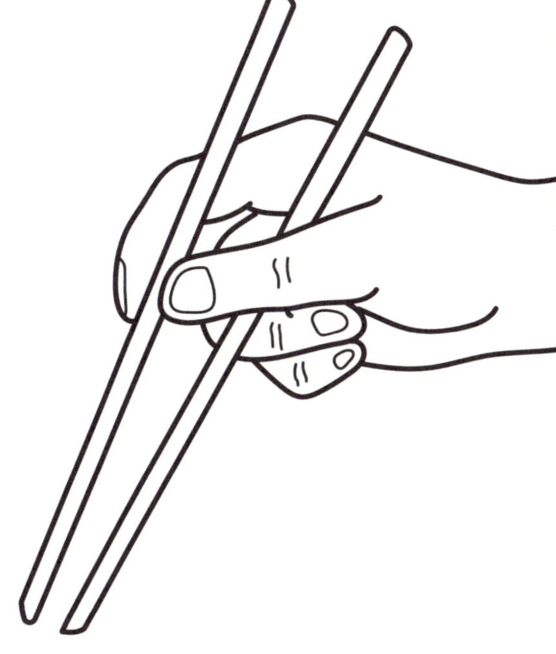

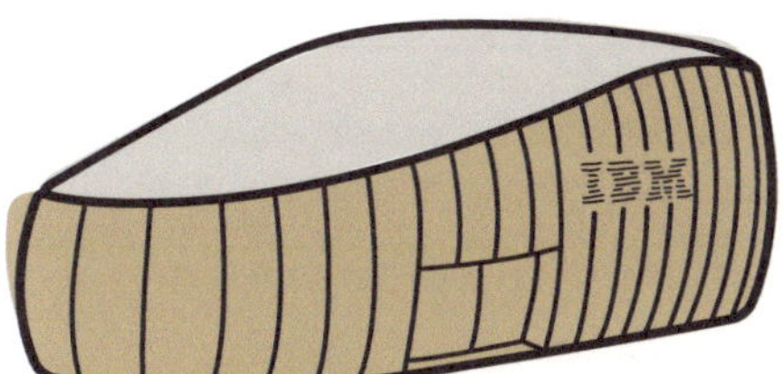

③ Piazza Tito Minniti

Very pleasant place surrounded by restaurants and food stores. I really enjoy the food market on saturday morning there.

Piazza Tito Minniti

To DRINK

④ Bar Frida

One of my favourite addresses of Isola. You should try their special Spritz Pompelmo Rosa or get some food, but you will also find a concept store and a exhibition space. The terrace is so cozy with its beautiful glass structure.

Via Antonio Pollaiuolo, 3

⑤ Aspirin Lifestyle

I enjoyed a lot this place to work and have a coffee. After long university sessions, have some piadine at the Paninoteca bar rigth next it.

Piazza Spotorno, 2

⑥ Lu po

I like the vibe of this place, nice decorations.

Via Francesco Arese, 20

⑦ Vinyl Pub

Nice bar in the lovely Piazzale Carlo Archinto. Really nice for summer nights.

Piazzale Carlo Archinto

⑧ Blue Note

The Blue Note is a nice cozy Jazz club, perfect to have a drink and enjoy some good music.

Via Pietro Borsieri, 37

⑨ Beer Show

I am not such a beer fan, but apparently this is the place to go if you want to enjoy beers in Milan.

Via Pietro Borsieri, 30

⑩ Bar Bah

Bar with a very nice athmosphere.

Via Luigi Porro Lambertenghi, 20

⑪ Type

Cheap but nice aperitivo place.

Via Pietro Borsieri, 34

To EAT

⑫ Nord Est Café

I love the vibe of this cafe. The waiters are really friendly and the restaurant offers typical daily dishes. Via Pietro Borsieri is now fully pedestrian so it is very pleasant to have lunch in a terrace.

Via Pietro Borsieri, 35

⑬ Assaje

One of the best pizzas I have eaten in Milan. You are welcomed with prosecco and they will offer some digestivo like pistacello, limoncello or meloncillo at the end. A safe choice!

Via Traù, 2

⑭ Gelateria Borsieri

After a nice lunch at cafe Nord Est, pass by this gelateria for a nice home made ice cream. Special mention to the stracciatella taste!

Via Pietro Borsieri, 25

⑮ Miscusi

Really nice pasta restaurant. The interior decoration makes a great athmosphere. Special mention to rigatoni carbonara and pesto tre colore.

Piazza Tito Minniti, 6

⑯ La Coccinella

Nice pizzeria in Piazza Tito Minniti.

Piazza Tito Minniti, 8

⑰ Mathara Ambula

Very good Sri Lankan cuisine.

Via Luigi Federico Menabrea, 2

 **To Party**

⑱ Alcatraz

This club is really huge. There are 3 different spaces : techno, reggaeton and commercial. This is also a concert place with good international programmation. A must see of Milan nightlife.

Via Valtellina, 25

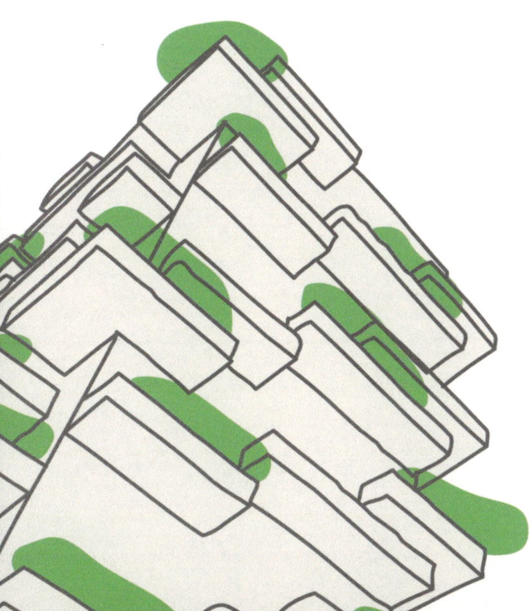

il bosco verticale

SAN LORENZO
1
2
3
4
5
6
7
8
9
10
10
11
12
13
14
SAN LORENZO

Located in the south of the city center, the district of San Lorenzo, Sant'Ambrogio and Guastalla are quieter compared to the hustle and bustle of the center. Unfortunately, I did not get the chance to explore them in depth, but I can still confirm there are some really nice spots to discover. Starting by **le colonne di San Lorenzo**, one of the main Roman ruins in Milan. A really good spot to enjoy an «Aperol d'asporto». Following **corso Ticinese**, you will find some of the city's best streetwear shops. Then, I would highly recommend to visit **la basilica Sant'Ambrogio,** and especially **la basilica Sant'Eufamia**, the prettiest church of Milan, in my opinion, with a wonderful blue ceiling. Then, finish your day with a diavola at **Pizza AM** and a fancy drink in **La Cerba**, one of my favorite spots to enjoy some good cocktails.

To See

① Colonne di San Lorenzo

Ruins of a Roman temple, the columns have been transported to the current location to complete la Basilica San Lorenzo, which is an impressive church to visit because of its tremendous height. It is also a great place to relax and have a drink.

Corso di Porta Ticinese, 39

② Parco Giovanni Paolo II

Located just behind la Basilica San Lorenzo, it is a nice park where you can escape from the crowd.

Via Vetere, 14

③ Basilica di Sant'Ambrogio

One of the oldest churches of Milan, I really like the composition of the entrance. Right next to it, you should have a look to the Università del Sacro Cuore. The inside is simply amazing to visit with the aula magna, an old monk canteen turned into a classroom.

Piazza Sant'Ambrogio, 15

④ Santuario di Sta. Maria dei Miracoli presso San Celso

It can bee seen as sant'Ambrogio little sister. You will find the same type of court at the entrance and a very beautiful interior work.

Corso Italia, 37

⑤ Il Dito

This surprising sculpture is facing la Borsa, a symbol against capitalism (despite the fact that the artist never provided any explicit explanation). Its real name is L.O.V.E., Liberta, Odio, Vendetta, Eternita.

P.za degli Affari

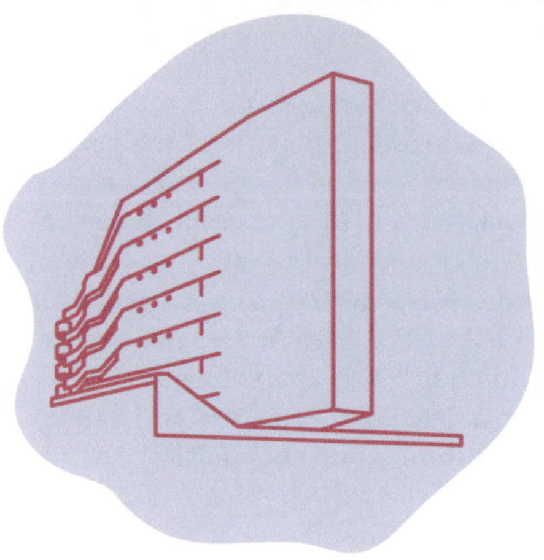

⑥ Basilica di Sant'Eufemia

Small church but outstanding for its wonderful interior decoration! The blue roof is simply amazing. Very nice discovery. Before visiting the church have a look at the original building Corso d'Italia by Luigi Moretti.

P.za Sant'Eufemia, 2

⑦ Rotonda della Besana

The architecture of this building is quite unique: a small park surrounded by arches in rotonda shape. Nice cultural events are sometimes organised inside.

Via Enrico Besana, 12

⑧ Via Torino

One of the most famous streets of Milan with the biggest fashion brands. Have a look to la chiesa di Santa Maria presso San Satiro and take a look to the choir. Surprising, isn't it?

Via Torino, 16-20

⑨ Pinacoteca Ambrosiana

Nice small museum featuring classic paintings (Caravagio, Da Vinci, Raphaelo…). The library inside is also remarkably beautiful.

Piazza Pio XI, 2

⑩ Corso di Porta Ticinese

Tiny street with plenty of trendy clothing shops and good restaurants. Just before joining Navigli, have a look to Basilica di Sant' Eustorgio.

Corso di Porta Ticinese

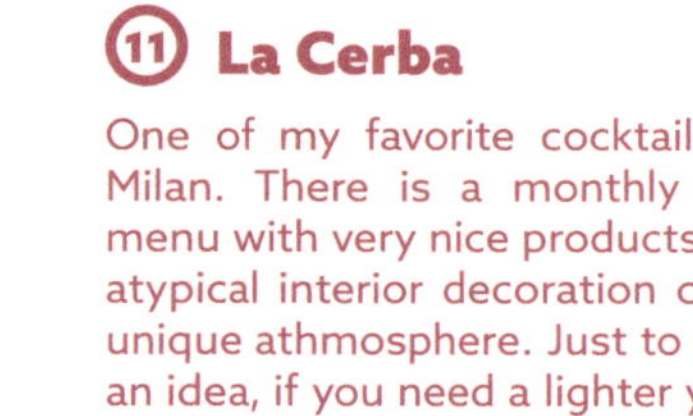

⑪ La Cerba

One of my favorite cocktail bars in Milan. There is a monthly cocktail menu with very nice products and the atypical interior decoration creates a unique athmosphere. Just to give you an idea, if you need a lighter you have one fixed to the door with a telescopic rope. Perfect place after a diavola at Pizza AM.

Via Orti, 4

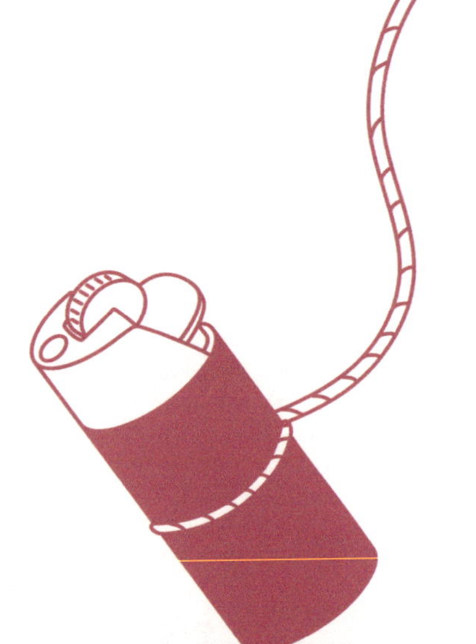

To **EAT**

⑫ Pizza AM

Very nice tiny restaurant. You are welcomed with a glass of prosecco and a slice of panzerotto.

Via Pietro Borsieri, 35

⑬ La Hora Feliz

One of the best price quality aperitivo places in Milan. Be fast if you want to have a slice of tiramisu!

Via Traù, 2

⑭ Farini

Nice d'asporto sliced pizza place.

Via Pietro Borsieri, 35

To **Party**

Sorry, sometimes you need to rest, no advice for this area. But be prepared for the next district!

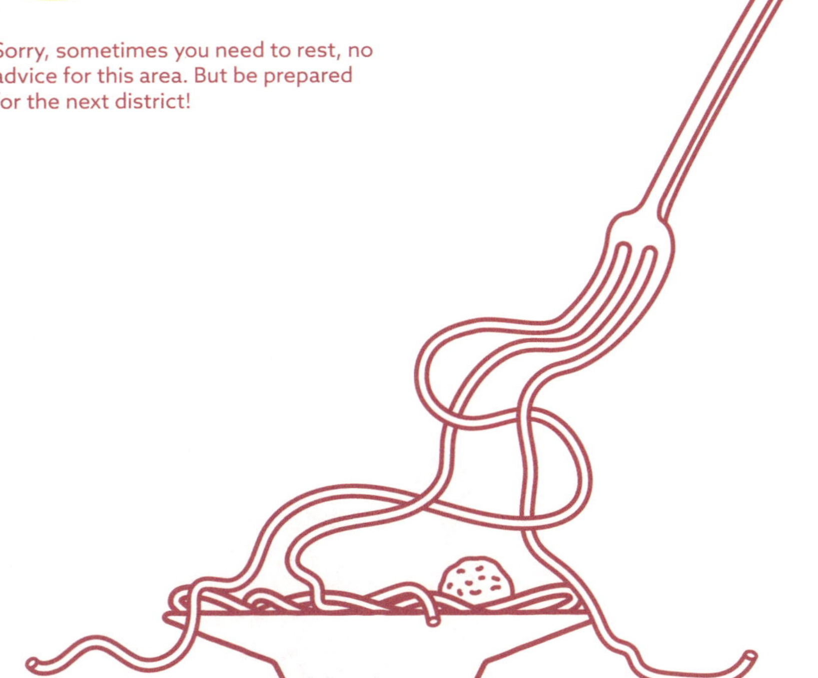

MONUMENTALE
1
9
7
4
10
3
5
2
8
6

mainly know this district for two main attractions : Il **Cimitero Monumentale** and **Chinatown**. I was surprised that visiting a cemetery could be a tourist activity, but I have to acknowledge that this one is really impressive because of its beauty , complexity and architectural design. If you are looking for less creepy experiences, I would suggest you to have a walk and dinner in Chinatown. This is the place for Asian food lovers in Milano.

Even if this area is mainly residential, there are some good spots to get some drinks (la **Chiesetta** and **Fabbrica 1928**) but also to enjoy some techno music until the end of the night in **Il tempio del futuro perduto**.

 **To See**

① Cimitero Monumentale

Might seem creepy to visit a cemetery but Cimitero Monumentale is special. There is a real architectural wealth for every memorial. Just have a look at the intensity of the blue found in the arches, just above Manzoni tomb. Outstanding!

Piazzale Cimitero Monumentale

② Chinatown

Second main attraction of this district, Chinatown is a very nice area to have a walk and enjoy some Asian food. I really like the chill vibe of this street.

Via Paolo Sarpi

③ ADI Design Museum

ADI is a museum dedicated to Italian design history. You will be able to see some design products and graphic design masterpieces, and attend exhibitions or talks.

Piazza Compasso d'Oro, 1

④ Fabbrica del Vapore

La Fabbrica del Vapore is an old railway depot converted into a cultural space where young artists can showcase their art. Check out the program online!

Piazza della Scala, 6

 **To DRINK**

⑤ La Chiesetta

Super small bar located in an old chapel. I really enjoyed this athmosphere.

Via Paolo Lomazzo, 12

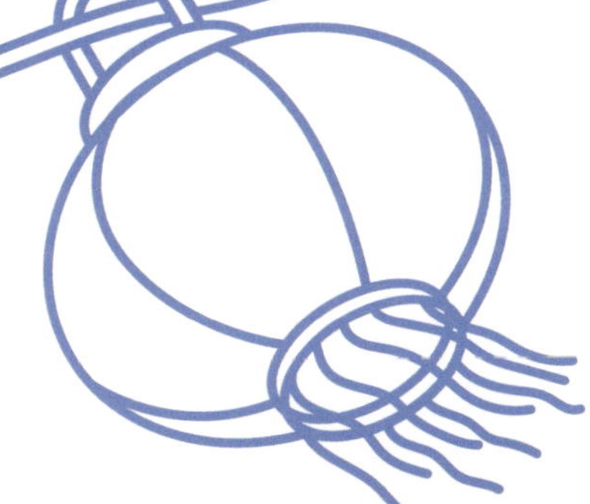

⑥ Via Cesare Cesariano

Street full of bars not far from Sempione. Everybody is drinking outside, which gives a cool vibe to the area.

Via Cesare Cesariano

⑦ Fabbrica 1928

This is the bar of La Fabbrica del Vapore complex. Nice place to have some food or a drink in the early evening with a cool industrial vibe.

Piazza della Scala, 6

To **EAT**

⑧ Via Paolo Sarpi

This is the main Chinatown street. I do not have a special restaurant recommandation but if you want to enjoy some Asian food, this is the place to go!

Via Pietro Borsieri, 35

To **Party**

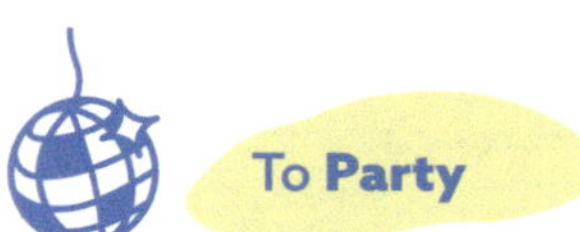

⑨ Tempio del Futuro Perduto

Really cool hybrid space. In the mornings, you can take some yoga/dance classes. During the afternoons, you can visit an art exhibition or go for a second hand market. At night, get some some «rest» at a techno dj set. The building is really nice and the garden is very pleasant, especially after a few dance moves.

Via Luigi Nono, 9/7

⑩ Il Gattopardo

The particularity of this club is its architecture: an old church where the altar has been turned into a bar counter. The music played is rather commercial.

Via Piero della Francesca, 47/51

BUENOS
AIRES
1
2
3
4
5
6
7
8
9
10

Buenos Aires / Porta Venezia are very young and dynamic districts. There is maybe not so much to see as a tourist, but they offer a nice nightlife, I would know. I enjoy to have some spritz in the crowded bars of **via Lecco**, but the place that stays in my memories is the mythic **Picchio**, an authentic family run bar. Amazing athmosphere and Negroni at 3€! After these pre-drinks, keep going until the end of the night in the **Tunnel club**.

The day after, if you are still hangover, do not hesitate to have a rest in the wonderful **Giardini Indro Montanelli**, a really nice park. If you still have some energy, visit **GAM** and explore its great classic painting collection. Not so well known but I have to say that it was one of my favorite museums in Milan. The building is amazing and you can see artists such as Van Gogh or Monet.

To **See**

① Giardini Indro Montanello

The second largest park after Sempione, I really love it. This is a relaxing place which offers some cultural options like natural history museum, the planetarium or Palazzo Dugnani.

Via Daniele Manin, 2

② GAM Galleria d'Arte Moderna

Maybe my favorite classic painting collection. Located in the amazing Villa Reale, this is a perfect human scale museum with artists such as Van Gogh, Manet, Filippini… During the summer, enjoy the garden of the villa.

Via Palestro, 16

③ Via Abramo Lincoln

Tiny and colorful street, which creates a vibrant contrast with the surrounding architecture.

Via Abramo Lincoln

④ Hangar Pirelli

Modern art museum in the north of Buenos Aires. This space is really huge and I have seen really interesting exhibitions. Check out the program online!

Via Chiese, 2

⑤ Villa Necchi Campiglio

Nice art deco villa located in the center of Milan. Close by, have a look at to the Liberty style architecture of the entrance of Casa Campanini or walk by via Bianca Maria to discover beautiful Milanese facades.

Via Mozart, 14

⑥ Picchio Bar

Definitely my favorite bar in Milan. This place is so authentic with pure chaos inside: at first glance, you do not really know if it is a Tabaccheria, a bar or a shop. This bar is often really crowded and you will be sure to meet some people. The family running the business is also really friendly and will not hesitate to make jokes or introduce you to random customers. Cocktails are really cheap, around 3,50€ each. And don't forget to bring an ID picture to stick it behind the bar. A must see!

Via Melzo, 11

⑦ Via Lecco

Street full of cheap bars with good vibes (such as the Red Cafè, for instance). It gets quite crowded during warm summer nights, best way to meet funny drunk people.

Via Lecco

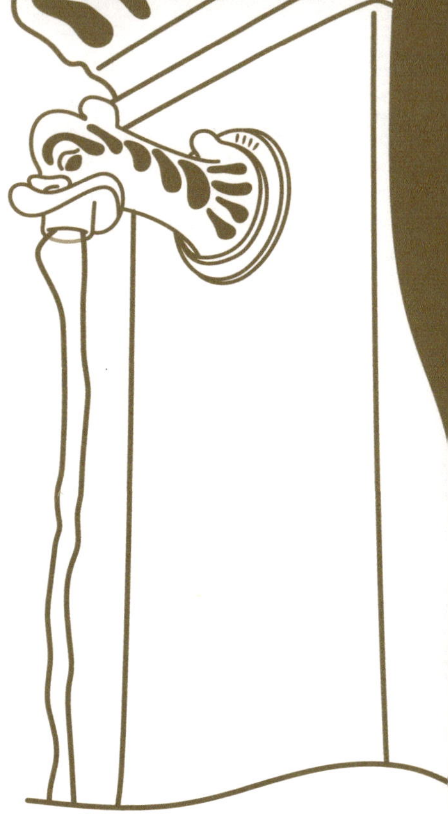

⑧ Pizzium

Nice pizza restaurant chain known for its thin crust.
Viale Tunisia, 6

⑨ Spontini

Another pizza restaurant chain, but this time known for its thick crust. That is really not my favorite pizza place, but it works for an after party snack.
Via Gaspare Spontini, 4

⑩ Tunnel club

Small and intimate club under the
rails, just north of the Milano central
station. Mainly playing electronic
music, but I went there for an Italian
indie party. Really nice vibes.

Via Giovanni Battista Sammartini, 30

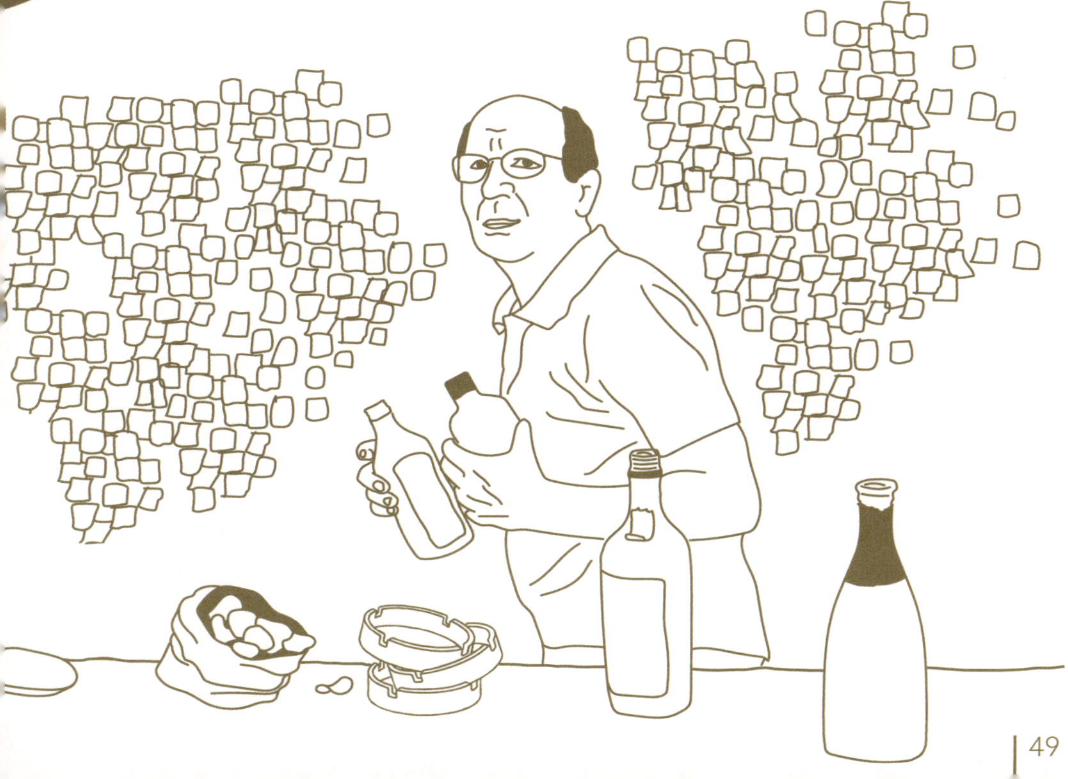

NAVIGLI
1
2
3
4
5
6
7
8
9
10
11
12
13
15
16
17
18

Navigli is the only place in Milan when you can sit by the two main canals of the city: **Navigli Grande** and **Navigli Pavese**. Many people gather here in the late afternoon, making it a great place for drinks during aperitivo time or for nights out (**Rocket club** for commercial lovers or **Apollo** for techno aficionados). In the summer, you can picnic in **Baden Powell** or **Segantini** parks.

Navigli is also known as a very dynamic artistic area for its modern art scene (**Mudec** or **Fondazione Prada**). You can also find places such as **Base** or **Ride Milano**, which combine cozy cafes with an exhibition space.

Towards the East, you also have some nice spots to go out with a chiller vibe like **Bagni misteriosi**, a swimming pool that turns into an orchestra aperitivo place during summer nights, or **Bachelite cLab**, a jazz bar.

To See

① Navigli

The start of the canal (Darsena) is a good spot to chill and have some drinks waiting for the sunset. Then, the main canal is full of aperitivo spots but often crowded. I would recommend you to go further to enjoy a peaceful walk.

Piazza Ventiquattro Maggio, 1

② MUDEC

MUDEC is a contemporary art museum with an incredible cloud like design at the entrance. It mainly hosts temporary exhibitions, so check online before going!
For info, via Tortona is a also a really nice place for aperitivo and restaurants.

Via Tortona, 56

③ Parco Baden Powell Parco Segantini

Nice park to have a picnic away from the crowds.

Parco Baden Powell / Segantini

④ Fondazione Prada

Another modern art museum in the South West of Milan. Its appeal depends on the current exhibition being showcased.

Via Giovanni Lorenzini, 10

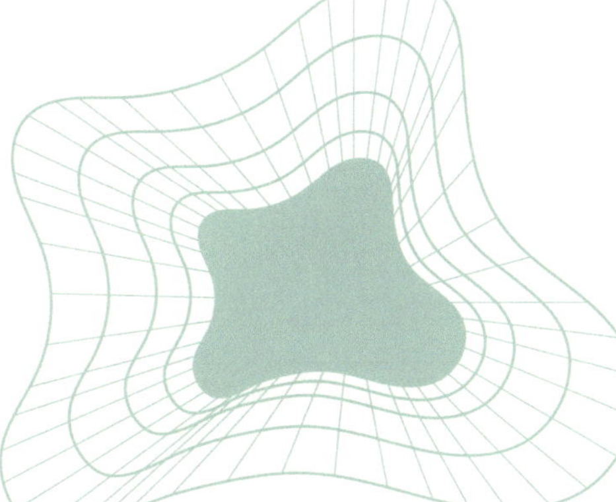

⑤ Universita Bocconi

New campus of the Milanese business school. I really like the modern
metal cloud structure. Good spot for
architecture lovers.

Via Gian Carlo Castelbarco, 27

⑥ Base

Really nice hybrid space. You will
be able to find some really good art
exhibitions while having some drinks
at the coffee place. It can also serve
as a pleasant workspace.

Via Bergognone, 34

⑦ Tenoha Cafe

Really nice spot to have a drink/work
in a cozy Japanese athmosphere. The
bar is also connected to a cool concept
store selling cool Japanese design products.

Via Vigevano, 18

⑧ Il Negozietto del gelato

Great gelateria on Navigli Pavese that
provides a quieter area to savor your
ice cream.

Alzaia Naviglio Pavese, 6

⑨ Bachelite cLab

Nice jazz bar. You can take your glass
outside and join the crowd in the
street to enjoy some good music.

Via Vertoiba, 3

⑩ Bagni Misteriosi

For summer nights, this swimming
pool is turned into an aperitivo place
where you can listen to a small orchestra playing on the water. The vibe there
is just great. I really recommend it but
you need to register on Facebook first!

Via Carlo Botta, 18

⑪ Vintage

An average aperitivo place, one of the cheapest in Via Ripa di Porta Ticinese.

Ripa di Porta Ticinese, 17

⑬ Locanda da Vinci

Very nice aperitivo place if you want to combine quality and price. The restaurant is located outside the main Navigli street, so you will be able to enjoy a peaceful terrace.

Alzaia Naviglio Pavese, 52

⑮ Bello Buono

Small restaurant, close by Porta Romana, inexpensive, excellent, only locals go there... a good sign!

Viale Sabotino, 14

⑫ A Vucciria

Nice Sicilian street food.

Viale Gorizia, 32A

⑭ Antica Pizzeria Fiorentina

« A hundred years old restaurant » with a warm welcome. All the soul of Italy in one place, for all your senses. Victim of its own success, some of the restaurant's dishes may not be available after 8pm. Prenota subito!

Viale Bligny, 41

⑯ Ride Milano

Ride is an excellent hybrid spot to get some drinks in Navigli. There is a nice terrace right next to the canal and a hangar. It can host either art exhibitions or transform into a club. It is one of my favorite addresses in Navigli.

Via Corsico, 3

⑰ Rocket club

Very nice club divided into 2 rooms: one more dedicated to Italian songs while the other plays more international music. The place is also quite cool, further from Navigli chaos.

Alzaia Naviglio Grande, 98

⑱ Apollo Club

Really nice place to enjoy techno music in a fancy environment.

Via Giosuè Borsi, 9/2

FASTWEB
CLOSE THE GAP
OPEN YOUR FUTURE

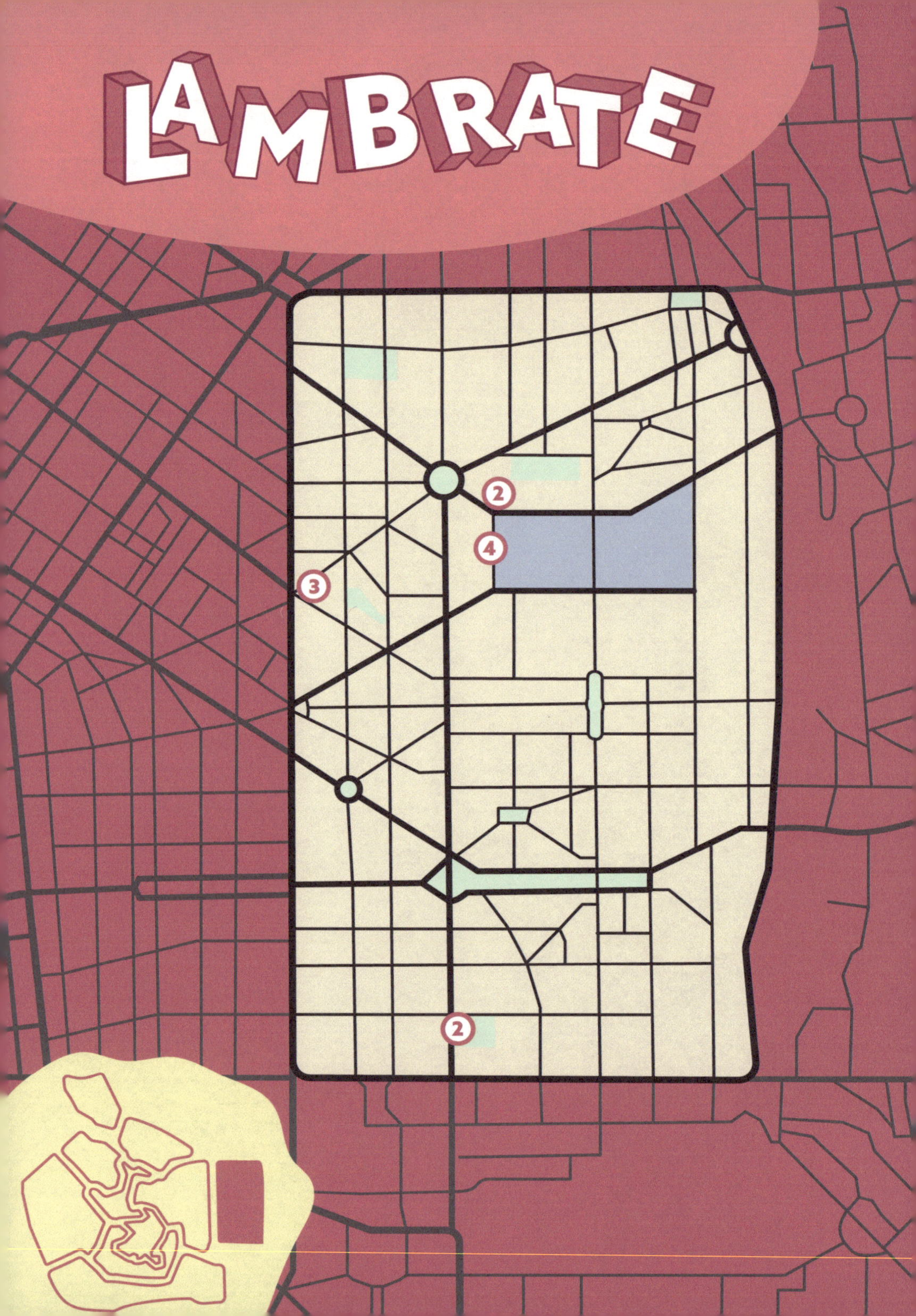

LAMBRATE
2
4
3
2

I did not get the chance to visit Lambrate so much since it is rather a quiet residential area. The few times I went, it was to enjoy some drink at aperitivo time in **Piazza Leonardo**, a cool place facing the emblematic **Politecnico campus**. But to be honest, I truly believe that it is a nice spot for leisurely walks and to discover some intimate bars or restaurants.

If you are still nostalgic of your student years, I would highly recommend to visit the Biblioteca Campus Leonardo right next to the **Green bar**. This is the architecture hub of PoliMi, and I loved passing by the desks to observe students working on building mock ups. However, if you are an alcoholic design lover, you must go to **Bar Basso** during il Salone del Mobile (design week) to taste the famous Negroni Sbagliato. You might meet some of the best designers in the world!

To **DRINK**

① Green Bar

Small coffee kiosk facing Biblioteca Campus Leonardo. Perfect coffee place after a long studying session.

Via Andrea Maria Ampère

③ Bar Basso

Bar Basso is one of the must see bars in Milan. Refuge of the best designers during design week, it is known as the bar where Negroni Sbagliato has been invented.

Via Plinio, 39

② Boom Milano

To be honest, I have never been to the bar, but the surroundings are pretty unusual. There is a giant dinosaur sculpture in the middle of the park. Take a moment to explore and you might be able to find the tail.

Viale Campania, 12

To **See**

④ Piazza Leonardo

Politecnico Leonardo Campus hosts the architecture and computer science facilities. At aperitivo time, you will most probably find a bunch of students enjoying a Spritz. Lovely vibe!

Piazza Sant'Ambrogio, 15

BOVISA
7
1
7
1
3
2

District where I spent the most time due to my master's studies. Bovisa is mainly known for hosting two campuses of **Politecnico di Milano**: to the East **La Masa**, the engineering hub and towards the West **Candiani**, the design area. The post industrial style of the buildings makes it a really interesting architectural complex. I truly enjoyed my time there and it gave me the opportunity to discover my passion for design. If you happen to visit it during graduation days, you might notice young students with a laurel crown celebrating their diploma while the crowds shout «Dottore».

Even if you are not pursuing further studies, the connecting street via Candiani is worth exploring for its rich street food culture. For pasta lovers, I strongly recommand **125**, a delicious authentic place with their well known pizzoccheri. Otherwise, grab a delicious focaccia to go at **Il Paradiso del Pane**.

To See

① Politecnico di Milano

The campus is split two parts: La Masa hosting the engineering campus and Candiani for design. I really loved my time in these buildings. The athmosphere in these post industrial buildings was really fostering our creativity. If you pass by, have a small drink in PolEatecnico.

Via Giuseppe Candiani, 72

② Parco Nicolo Savarino

Nice park in the neighbourhood of Maciachini. The perfect starting point for a 10km run around parco Nord.

Via Livigno

③ Nuovo Armenia

I have never been to this cultural space but I have been told that they have some very cool events such as independent movie projections.

Via Livigno, 9

④ Dolci Storie

Suuuuuuper nice gelateria close by piazza Bausan. Special mention to pistachio flavour!

Via degli Imbriani, 47-51

⑤ PolEATechnico

Bar located in the middle of the design campus. Cheap drinks, nice vibes, perfect to relax after a lecture. Not only open to students, so have a look!

Via Giuseppe Candiani, 72

⑥ Vulkania

Really good authentic pizzeria in the center of Maciachini.

Via Valtellina, 63

⑦ Ti amo pizza

Small good pizzeria in Maciachini with a charismatic pizzaiolo.

Viale Edoardo Jenner, 10

⑧ 125

Candiani is the main road linking engineering to design campus and is well known by students to be the temple of street food restaurants. Among them, 125 was my favorite pasta place, the GOAT. Inside, you will discover a tiny local restaurant owned by a friendly team of chefs. Special mention to trofie alle noci and pizzoccheri, the famous mountain pasta.

Via Giuseppe Candiani, 125

⑨ Il Paradiso del Pane

Nice and authentic panino place next to the design campus. They have cheap focaccia and panzerotti. Special mention to the pasticciotto al limone!

Via Don Giovanni Verità, 19

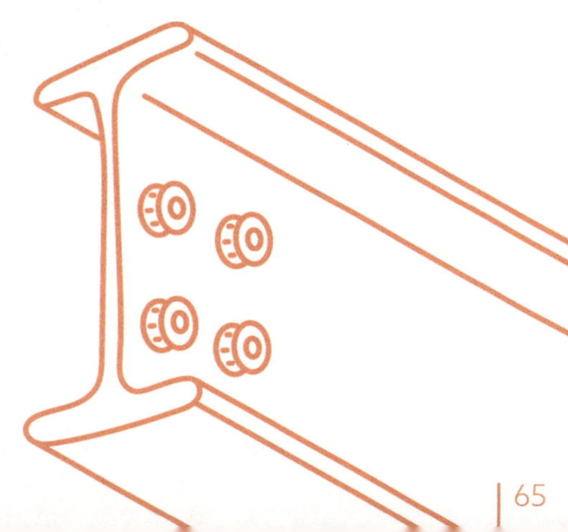

10 Pasta Mi

Another good spot to enjoy Italian pasta in the Candiani area.

Via Giuseppe Candiani, 101

11 Scudo Cafe

Good classical Italian café with nice piadine.

Via Giuseppe Candiani, 98

To Party

12 Spirit of Milan

Spirit of Milan is an old industrial building housing a bar, a restaurant and a concert hall. Although I have never been there, I have been told that it's a nice place to grab some food and enjoy some live music. It looks really cool indeed!

Via Bovisasca, 57/59

TRE
TORRI
5
6
1
3
4
2

Tre Torri, also known as **City Life** is another great example illustrating how well the integration of modern architecture is a success in this city. You will be able to witness some of the most outstanding buildings of the Lombardian capital. Starting with the three towers that forms «Tre Torri» featuring worldclass architectural structures such as Zaha Hadid's iconic curved Generali Tower or the unconventional Milano Congressi. City Life area also hosts charming residences that contribute to the modernist urban landscape.

This part of the city is also rich in history with one of the most famous paintings in the world: Il **Cenacolo di Da Vinci**. Please book tickets in advance, so you don't miss the opportunity to see this masterpiece.

Last but not least, I cannot forget to mention the heart of Milanese sport life, **San Siro** stadium hosting football games of both AC Milan and Inter. Do not miss the chance to live this authentic Milanese experience, purely unforgettable.

To See

① Tre Torri

Inside the complex of City Life, it migth be hard to miss the «Three towers»: the Isozaki tower is the most simple with its rectangular shape and a panoramic lift; the Crooked, my favorite, made by Zaha Hadid; and the Libeskind tower, very impressive for its curved shape.
Right down the towers, you will find a nice park where I enjoyed chilling and admiring the modern architecture.

Via Giuseppe Candiani, 72

② Chiesa Santa Maria della Grazie

This church is part of a dominican monastery of 15th century. I really enjoy the style of the dome. Once you have visited it, have a look at the details of the back facade. I really enjoyed its pastel palette.

Piazza di Santa Maria delle Grazie

③ Cenacolo

Rigth next to Santa Maria delle Grazie, you will be able to visit the Last Supper made by Leonardo da Vinci. Please book your tickets in advance to enjoy the 15 minutes you have to admire the painting.

Piazza di Santa Maria delle Grazie, 2

④ Cadorna

By itself, this station has nothing special to offer. You will have to have a look outside to be able to notice the unique sculpture Needle, Thread and Knot. The meaning is quite interesting: the needle pulling thread represents a train going through a tunnel or it can be a methaphor of a snake around a sword, which is the emblem of the city. It can also be interpreted as a tribute to Milan's fashion industry.

Piazzale Luigi Cadorna

⑤ San Siro - Giuseppe Meazza

Football is very rooted into Italian culture, and San Siro is maybe one of the most emblematic stadiums of this boot shape country. I have been there twice and the atmosphere is just amazing! The view of the pitch is outstanding and I loved the shape of the columns. If you have the chance to go for an AC Milan game, don't miss the «Sarà perche ti amo» a cappella before the game.

Piazzale Angelo Moratti

To **EAT**

⑥ City Life

To be honest, this is definetly not the most authentic place in Milan, but it is rather nice to grab some food and eat it in the park. You will mainly find Italian food chains such as Panini Durini or la Piadineria. Might be a detail, but I really like the shape of the roof of the mall, as an interesting design element.

Piazza Tre Torri

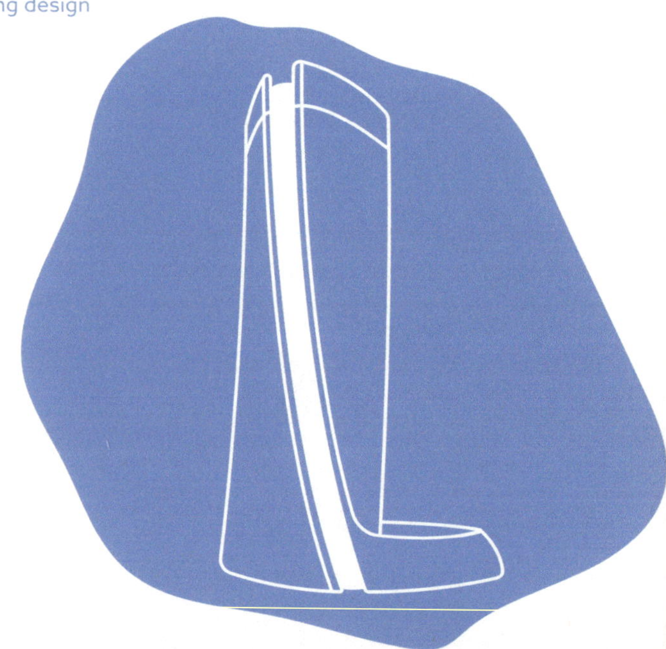

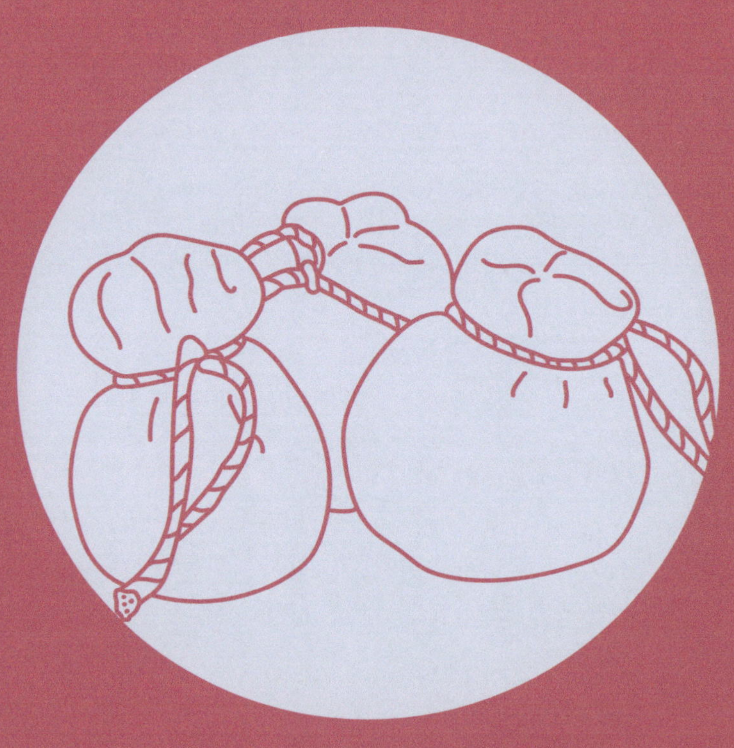

Outside
Milan

OUTSIDE
3
6
5
8
4
2
11
1
9
7
10
12

Even if Milan can be considered as its main attraction, the north of Italy has way more to offer : good food, beautiful landscape, nice Italian architecture... I will try to share with you my best discoveries that are easily accessible by trains from the Lombardian capital.

① Pavia 30min

If you are not a fan of Milanese modernism, Pavia will offer you the classic narrow streets, pastel color facades or small tipical bars... This is one of my favorite discoveries outside Milan. Have a walk through the city to discover the university's architecture, have a coffee close by the outstanding Duomo or just reach the bridge to experience Pavia from a different spot.

② Monza 30min

Monza's main attraction is its park, hosting every year a Formula 1 race, but it is also a very peaceful place to chill under the sun. The city center is also worth visiting with its beautiful Duomo facade.

③ Como Lake 30min

This area offers beautiful viewpoints in between mountains and water with some really nice hiking tracks (Monte Bolleto). After some physical efforts, have a coffee in one of the cute cities surrounding the lake such as Varese or Como. It is also possible have a dip there, but it is often very busy, so I would advise to go to Lecco which is less known.

④ Lago d'Orta 3h

Orta is definitely not the most famous lake of the region, but it is my favorite. Less crowed, it offers some beautiful spots to swim or enjoy a chill afternoon in the city of Orta San Giuliano.

⑤ Lago d'Iseo - Brescia 3h

Lago d'Iseo is special because it has an island in its center. It is a very nice hiking spot, with a breath taking view on the Alps peaks.
Before starting the hike, take the opportunity to spend some time in Brescia to visit this very cute city.

⑥ Bergamo 1h

The city is divided in 2 parts : «La citta bassa», the rather modern area, whereas uphill, the fortified Bergamo offers a medieval city center with beautiful viewpoints. Definitely worth visiting! If you stay more than a day, explore the mountains and pass by Selvino, a small village with nice hiking paths.

⑦ Parme - Modene 2h

These are 2 medium size cities that are nice to visit for a day only. In Parma, I have been amazed by the remains of wood made theater in Palazzo della Pilotta. For a tipical horse meat sandwich, go to Da Walter or Da Pepen.
Both city have a pretty city center worth visiting.

⑧ **Verona**   1h

Verona is known as the city of Romeo and Giuletta and despite the fact that Capulet's house is a rather touristic attraction, the city offers a rich and beautiful historical center. For an optimal sunset experience, grab a pizza at Redentore and eat it close by il Castel San Pietro to observe the city surrounding by the Adige. If you stay longer, I highly recommend to buy tickets for an open air orchestra in the Roman arena.

⑨ **Torino**   1h

The rivalry between Torino and Milan goes further than football. In addition, the two compete to be the best city in Lombardia. I am not the best person to give an objective answer, but Torino is a nice place to visit. The city center, dominated by the Mole Antonelliana, has a chiller vibe than Milan. I would highly recommand you to reach il Monte dei Cappuccini to admire the city from the heights.

⑩ **Bologna**   1h

If you have the chance to go to Bologna, do not miss the chance to try some authentic Bolognese pasta at Capra e Cavoli. Then, after passing by Piazza Maggiore or the 2 towers, follow the arches and reach il Santuario Madonna di San Luca to enjoy the view on the country side or the unusual architecture of il stadio Dall'Ara.

⑪ **Mantova - Cremona** 3h

These are 2 beautiful tipical Italian cities perfect for a day visit. If Cremona is well known for the quality of its violins, it also has a very nice duomo to visit. I definitely recommend spending a day in the small «peninsula» of Mantova. Indeed, the city is surrounded by il Lago di Mezzo and offers a really beautiful architecture. Enter in Basilica di Sant'Andrea or il Palazzo Ducale before walking along the banks of the city for some snacks. If you still have some time, I would suggest to pass by Crema, the city where «Call Me by Your Name» has been shot and Piacenza, a quiet but really cute city.

⑫ **Ligurian cost** 3h
Genova/Portofino/Santa Maria

To finish with this trip around the North of Italy, I would suggest you to reach the Mediterranean sea. If I am not such a fan of the very industrial Genova, I really like all the Ligurian coast up to Rapallo. There are so many nice villages to discover with cute pastel city centers. During the quiet touristic season, I would really recommand hiking around Portofino to admire the sea, but bring your own sandwich to avoid spending money for lunch !

Lecco

Lago d'Orta

— **Mountains around Bergamo**

Portofino

Bologna

4
Indie
Italiano

Their milanese experience has been the opportunity to discover a new music genre : **l'indie italiano**. I discovered so many talented artists that deserve a better recognition worldwide. This page is an hommage to the singers that have produced the soundtrack of my Italian journey. And in case you would fall in love with this genre too, don't hesitate to join **Mi A Mi**, the indie music festival organised in May in Milano.

Franco 126

Stanza Singola (ft Tommaso Paradiso) • Brioschi • Nuvole di drago • Vabbé • Nessun perché • Simone • Miopia • Che senso ha • Marciapiedi • Quante notti • Tutto fuori controllo

Frah **Quintale**

8 miliardi di persone • Due ali • Sotto effetto • Nei treni la notte • Hai visto mai • Si, ah • Gli occhi • Cratere • Missili • Gravita • Gabbiani • Si puo darsi • Alta marea

Laila **Al Habash**

Brodo • Flambé • Ponza • Paranoia • Gelosa • Soffice • Giove

Canova

Manzarek • Ho capito che non eravamo • 14 sigarette • Lento violento

Calcutta

Se piovesse il tuo nome • Parace-
tamolo • Sorriso • Gaetano • Frosi-
none • Del verde • Briciole • Pesto •
Kiwi • Oroscopo • Non esiste amore
a Napoli • Controtempo

Giuse The Lizia

Vietnam • Particelle (ft Laila Al
habast) • Segretaria • Ricomincio da
tre • Lato A Lato B • Boy, don't cry •
Giorni Blue • Il brutto del mondo •
Sincera • Gocce sugli occhi • Ricomincio da tre • Radical

Venerus

Love anthem, No1 • Senza di me (ft
Franco 126 & Gemitaiz) • Altrove •
Forse ancora dorme • Canzone per
un amico • Non vivo piu sulla terra
• Buonanotte

Willie Peyote

Ottima Scusa • La tua futura ex mo-
glie • C'era una vodka • Che bella
Giornata • Cuando nessuno ti vede
• My bad • Vermi • Semaforo

Coez

Domenica • E sempre bello • La musica non c'è • Faccio un casino • La tua canzone • non odiare mai • Davide • Faccio un casino • Le luci della città

RKomi

Blu (feat Elisa) • La coda del diavolo • Partire da te • Insuperabile • Mai piu • Acqua calda e limone (feat Ernia)

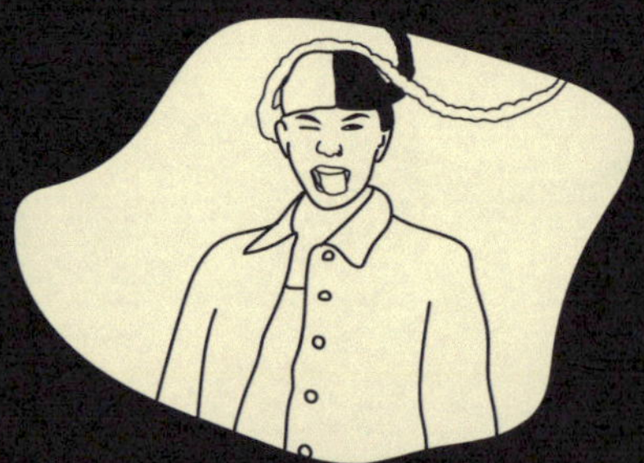

VV

Cheerios • Paranoie • Antidoto • Felicità • La domenica sul divano • Vita lenta

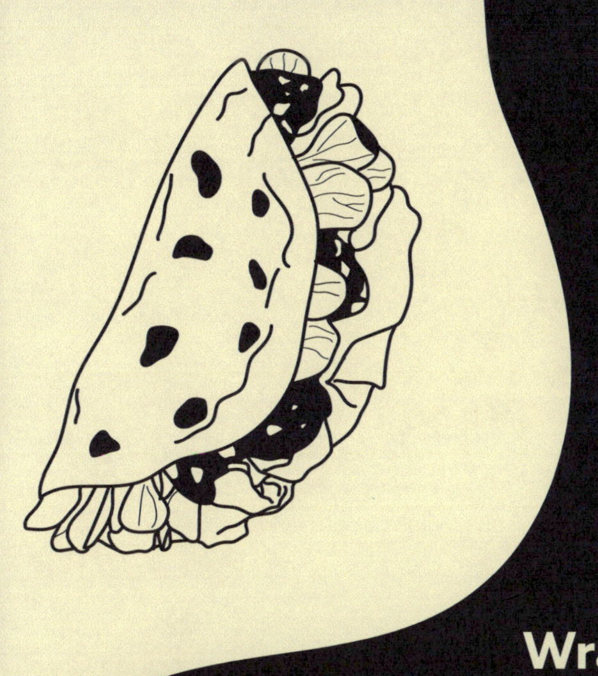

Wrap
Some extra song «in vrac»

Nico LaOnda - Fratello gemma
Ariete - L
Postino - Blu
Memento - A volte mi perdo
Galeffi - Occhiaie
Fabri Fibra - Stavo pensando a te
Labadessa - Non me lo so spiegare
Rokas - Giorni stupidi
Bnkr44 - Aquiloni
Vipra - Baby Mama
Gemitaiz - La prossima volta
Gemitaiz - Colpevole
Gemitaiz - Restiamo soli
Fulminacci - Meglio di cosi
Fulminacci - Brutte compagnie
Mazzariello - Pubblicità progresso
Madame - Aranciata
Madame - Donna Vedi
Elex - Cinico
MACE - Mai piu

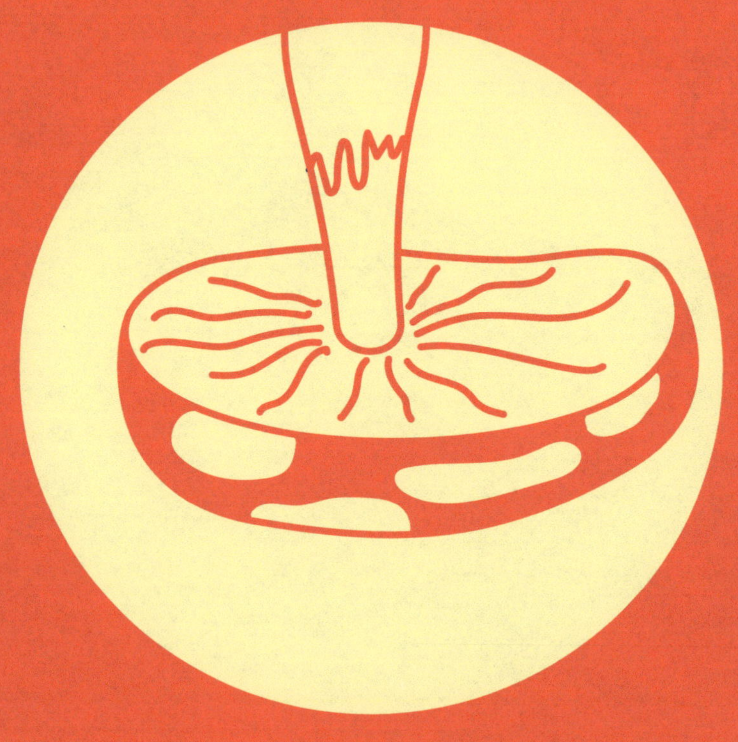

La vostra
Milano

Thanks to this book, you might also have the chance to discover other unique spots in Milan, by losing yourself in the endless streets of the city. Then, this page is yours! I invite you to gather your best addresses here to create your version of Milan. Enjoy!

to See

to Party

to Drink

to Eat

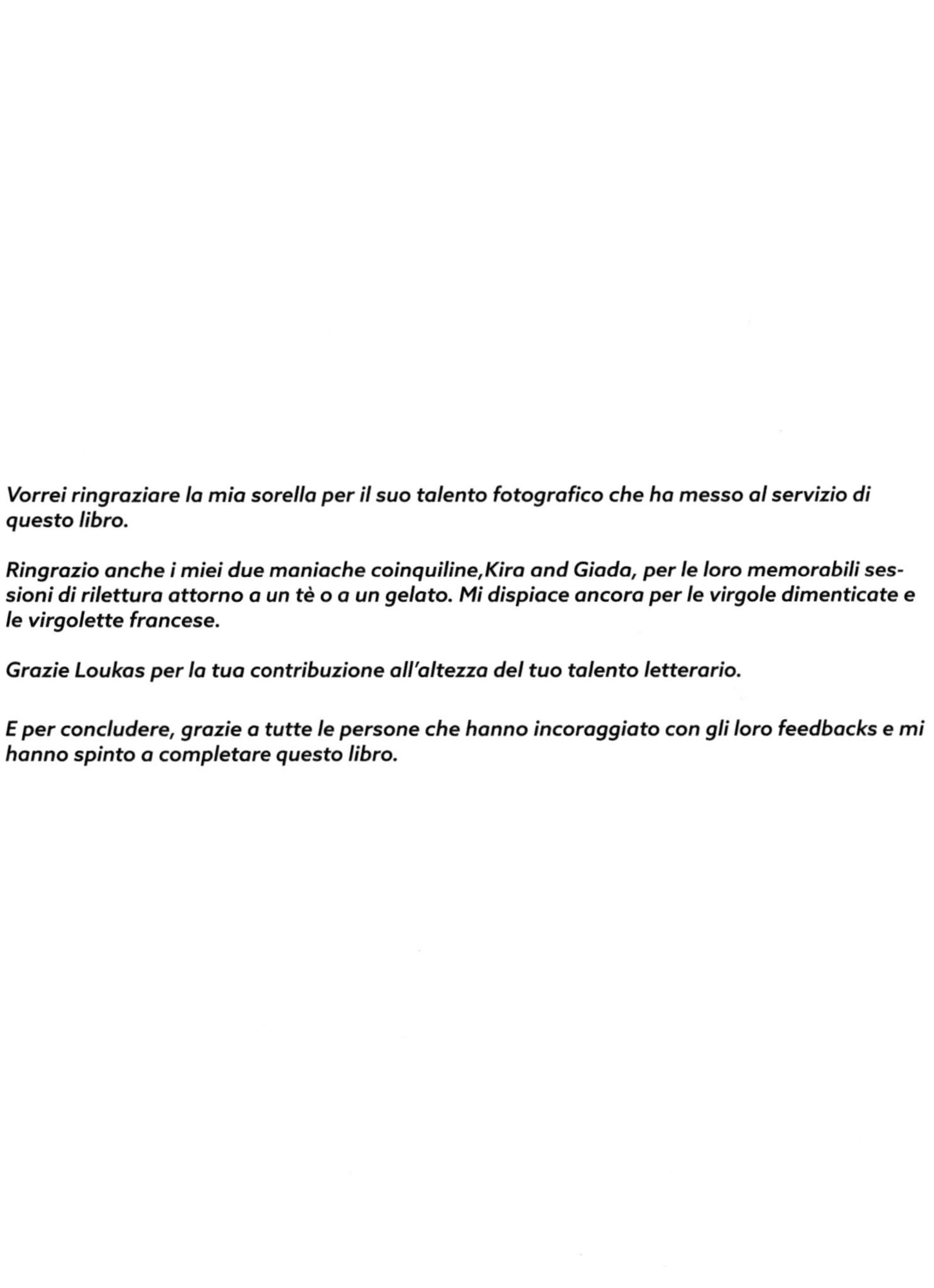

Vorrei ringraziare la mia sorella per il suo talento fotografico che ha messo al servizio di questo libro.

Ringrazio anche i miei due maniache coinquiline,Kira and Giada, per le loro memorabili sessioni di rilettura attorno a un tè o a un gelato. Mi dispiace ancora per le virgole dimenticate e le virgolette francese.

Grazie Loukas per la tua contribuzione all'altezza del tuo talento letterario.

E per concludere, grazie a tutte le persone che hanno incoraggiato con gli loro feedbacks e mi hanno spinto a completare questo libro.

© 2024 Antoine Simminger
Édition : BoD - Books on Demand, info@bod.fr
Impression : BoD - Books on Demand, In de
Tarpen 42, Norderstedt (Allemagne)
Impression à la demande
ISBN : 978-2-3225-3936-9
Dépôt légal : juin 2024